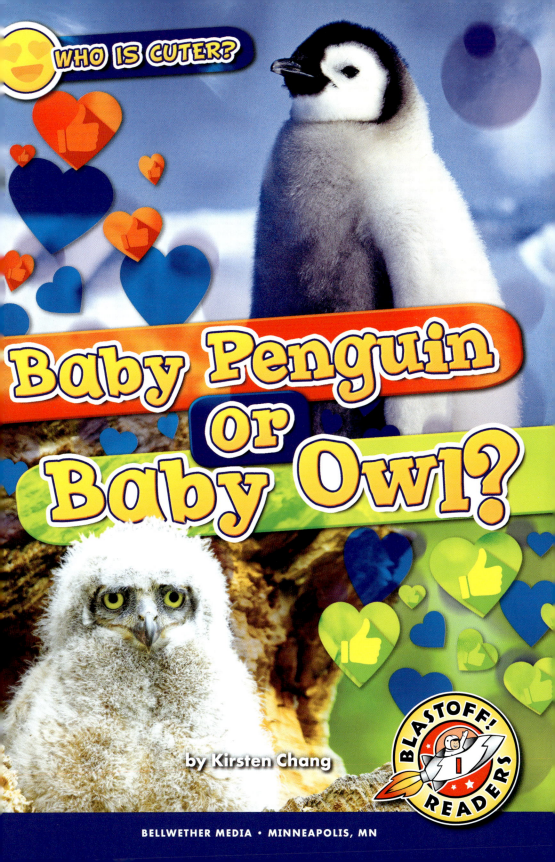

Blastoff! Readers are carefully developed by literacy experts to build reading stamina and move students toward fluency by combining standards-based content with developmentally appropriate text.

 Level 1 provides the most support through repetition of high-frequency words, light text, predictable sentence patterns, and strong visual support.

 Level 2 offers early readers a bit more challenge through varied sentences, increased text load, and text-supportive special features.

 Level 3 advances early-fluent readers toward fluency through increased text load, less reliance on photos, advancing concepts, longer sentences, and more complex special features.

★ **Blastoff! Universe**

This edition first published in 2025 by Bellwether Media, Inc.

No part of this publication may be reproduced in whole or in part without written permission of the publisher. For information regarding permission, write to Bellwether Media, Inc., Attention: Permissions Department, 6012 Blue Circle Drive, Minnetonka, MN 55343.

Library of Congress Cataloging-in-Publication Data

Names: Chang, Kirsten, 1991- author.
Title: Baby penguin or baby owl? / by Kirsten Chang.
Description: Minneapolis, MN : Bellwether Media, Inc., 2025. | Series: Blastoff! Readers: who is cuter? | Includes bibliographical references and index. | Audience term: Children | Audience term: School children | Audience: Ages 5-8 | Audience: Grades K-1 | Summary: "Developed by literacy experts for students in kindergarten through grade three, this book introduces baby penguins and baby owls to young readers through leveled text and related photos" -Provided by publisher.
Identifiers: LCCN 2024034988 (print) | LCCN 2024034989 (ebook) | ISBN 9798893042269 (library binding) | ISBN 9798893044058 (paperback) | ISBN 9798893043235 (ebook)
Subjects: LCSH: Penguins–Infancy–Juvenile literature. | Owls–Infancy–Juvenile literature.
Classification: LCC QL676.2 .C43 2025 (print) | LCC QL676.2 (ebook) | DDC 598.13/92–dc23/eng/20240802
LC record available at https://lccn.loc.gov/2024034988
LC ebook record available at https://lccn.loc.gov/2024034989

Text copyright © 2025 by Bellwether Media, Inc. BLASTOFF! READERS and associated logos are trademarks and/or registered trademarks of Bellwether Media, Inc.

Editor: Rachael Barnes   Designer: Andrea Schneider

Printed in the United States of America, North Mankato, MN.

Table of Contents

Chicks and Owlets	4
Webbed Feet and Talons	8
Swim and Fly	14
Who Is Cuter?	20
Glossary	22
To Learn More	23
Index	24

Chicks and Owlets

Penguins and owls are birds. Baby penguins are chicks. Baby owls are owlets.

chicks

owlets

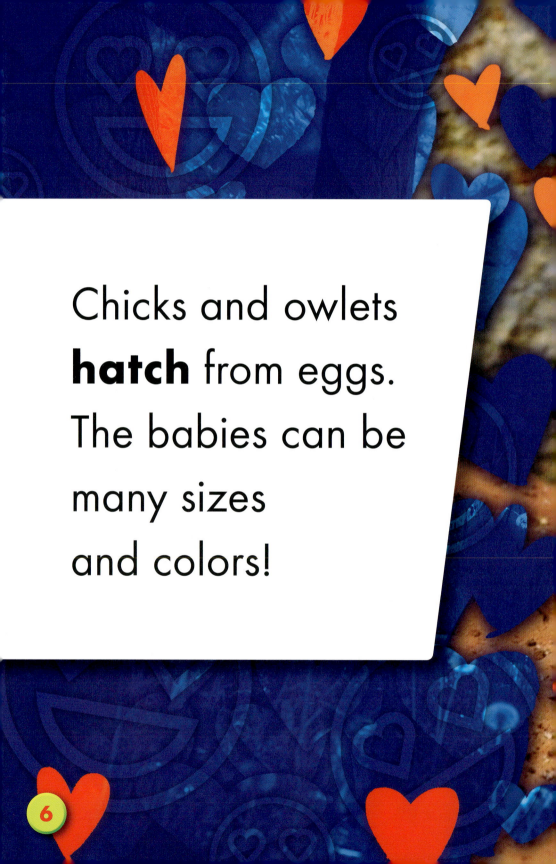

Chicks and owlets **hatch** from eggs. The babies can be many sizes and colors!

Webbed Feet and Talons

Chicks have **webbed feet**. Owlets have sharp **talons**.

Both babies have special eyes. Chicks can see underwater. Owlets can see well at night.

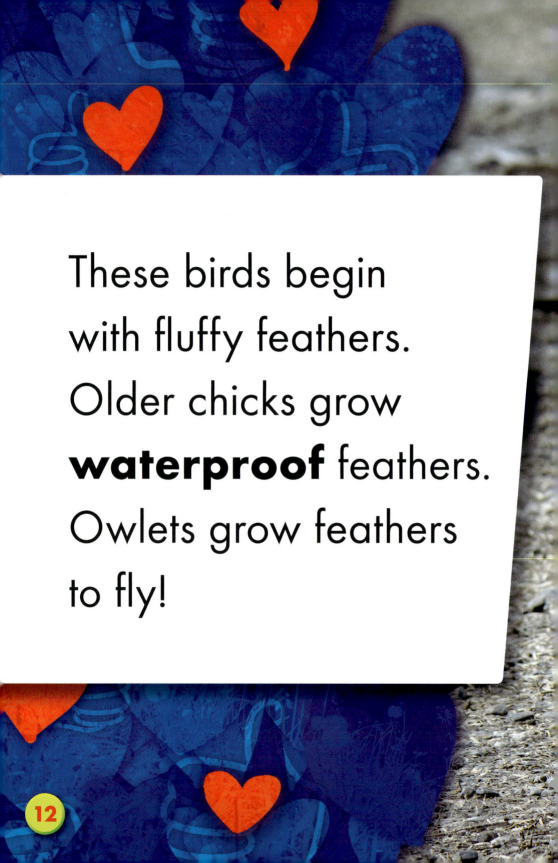

These birds begin with fluffy feathers. Older chicks grow **waterproof** feathers. Owlets grow feathers to fly!

fluffy feathers

Swim and Fly

These babies start to move on their own. Chicks **waddle**. Owlets hop and climb.

waddling

15

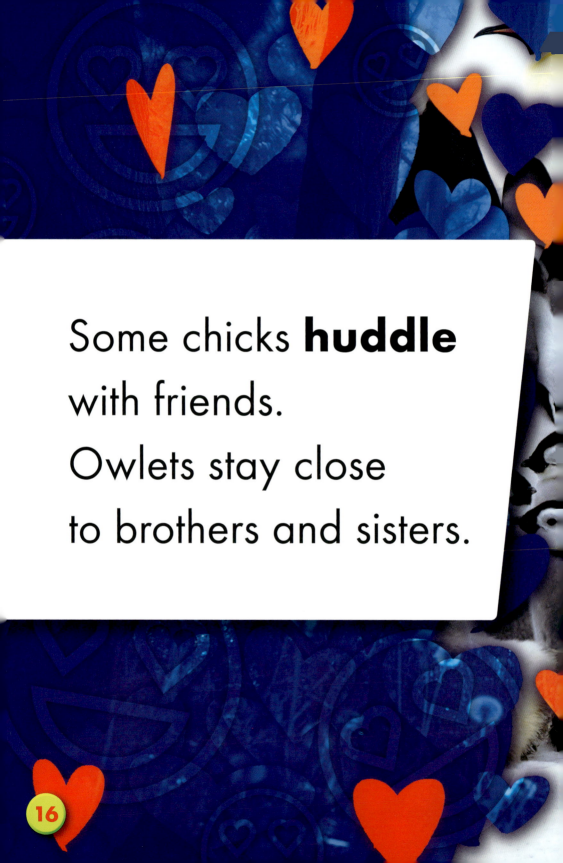

Some chicks **huddle** with friends. Owlets stay close to brothers and sisters.

huddling

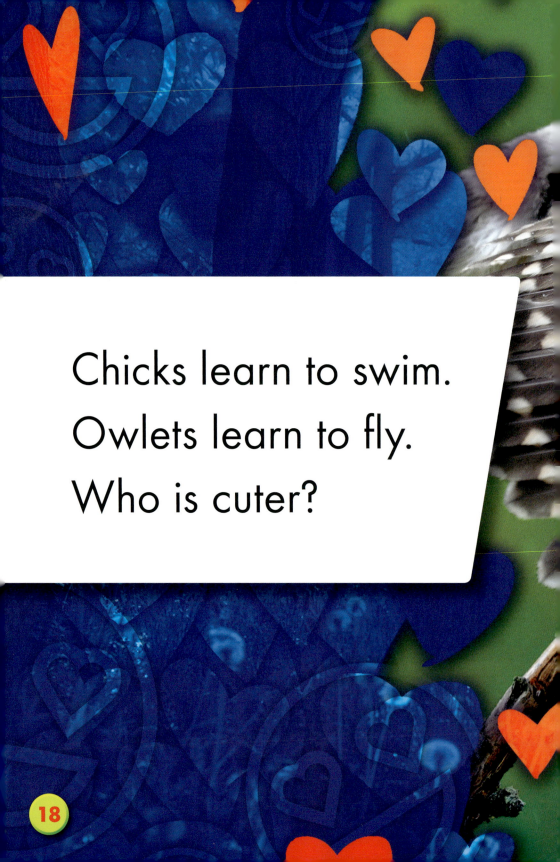

Chicks learn to swim.
Owlets learn to fly.
Who is cuter?

Who Is Cuter?

eyes for seeing underwater

waterproof feathers

webbed feet

Baby Penguin

waddles

huddles with friends

swims

eyes for seeing at night

feathers for flying

talons

Who is your pick? Vote at BellwetherMedia.com

Baby Owl

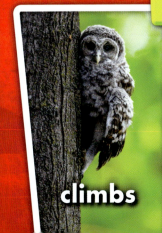
climbs

stays close to brothers and sisters

flies

Glossary

hatch

to break out of an egg

waddle

to walk by moving from side to side

huddle
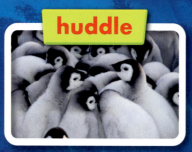
to gather close together for warmth

waterproof
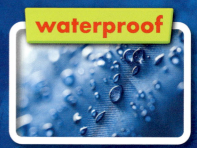
able to stay dry in wet areas

talons

the strong, sharp claws of owls

webbed feet

feet with thin skin between the toes

To Learn More

AT THE LIBRARY

Carney, Elizabeth. *Forest Babies*. Washington, D.C.: National Geographic Kids, 2023.

Horning, Nicole. *Baby Penguins*. New York, N.Y.: Cavendish Square Publishing, 2021.

Rustad, Martha E. H. *All About Baby Penguins*. North Mankato, Minn.: Pebble, 2022.

ON THE WEB

FACTSURFER

Factsurfer.com gives you a safe, fun way to find more information.

1. Go to www.factsurfer.com.

2. Enter "baby penguin or baby owl" into the search box and click 🔍.

3. Select your book cover to see a list of related content.

Index

birds, 4, 12
climb, 14
colors, 6
eggs, 6, 7
eyes, 10
feathers, 12, 13
fly, 12, 18
hatch, 6, 7
hop, 14
huddle, 16, 17
night, 10
owls, 4
penguins, 4
sizes, 6
swim, 18
talons, 8, 9
underwater, 10
waddle, 14, 15
webbed feet, 8, 9

The images in this book are reproduced through the courtesy of: John Conrad/ Getty Images, front cover (penguin); TPCImagery - Mike Jackson, front cover (owl); Charles Bergman, pp. 3 (penguin), 15 (waddling); Eric Isselee, pp. 3 (owl), 21 (owl); vladsilver, pp. 4-5 (chicks), 20 (huddles); Kurit afshen, pp. 5 (owlets), 22 (talons); Krys Bailey/ Alamy, pp. 6-7; webguzs, p. 7 (chick hatching); Design Pics Inc/ Alamy, pp. 8-9; Raymond Hennessy/ Alamy, p. 9 (talons); Ann and Steve Toon/ Alamy, pp. 10-11; Nick Rule/ Alamy, p. 11; knelson20, pp. 12-13; Jim Cumming, p. 13; Ahmed Abubasel, pp. 14-15; Danita Delimont/ Alamy, pp. 16-17; Chase D'animulls, p. 17; David Tipling, p. 19; Cindy Hopkins/ Alamy, p. 20 (penguin); Alamy, p. 20 (waddles); Giedrius Stakauskas/ Alamy, p. 20 (swims); FotoRequest, p. 21 (climbs); Andrew Glogower, p. 21 (stays close to brothers and sisters); Victor Tyakht/ Alamy, p. 22 (hatch); Fuse/ Getty Images, p. 22 (huddle); © Ndp | Dreamstime.com, p. 22 (waddle); chaphot, p. 22 (waterproof); Kim Marriott/ Alamy, p. 22 (webbed feet).